THE G.I. SERIES

America's Commandos

A Paramarine armed with a Reising SMG and a Colt pistol. He is kitted out in the distinctive jump smock. (IWM)

THE G.I. SERIES

THE ILLUSTRATED HISTORY OF THE AMERICAN SOLDIER, HIS UNIFORM AND HIS EQUIPMENT

America's Commandos

U.S. Special Operations Forces of World War II and Korea

Leroy Thompson

Pen & Sword
MILITARY

*America's Commandos: U.S. Special Operations Forces
of World War II and Korea*

A Greenhill Book
First published in 2001 by Greenhill Books,
Lionel Leventhal Limited
www.greenhillbooks.com

This edition published in 2015 by
PEN & SWORD MILITARY
An imprint of
Pen & Sword Books Ltd
47 Church Street
Barnsley
South Yorkshire
S70 2AS

Copyright © Lionel Leventhal Limited, 2001

ISBN: 978-1-84832-805-1

The right of Leroy Thompson to be identified as
Author of this work has been asserted by him in
accordance with the Copyright, Designs and
Patents Act 1988.

CIP data records for this title are available from
the British Library.

Designed by DAG Publications Ltd
Design by David Gibbons
Layout by Anthony A. Evans

Printed and bound in Malta by Gutenberg Press Ltd

Pen & Sword Books Ltd incorporates the Imprints
of Aviation, Atlas, Family History, Fiction, Maritime,
Military, Discovery, Politics, History, Archaeology,
Select, Wharncliffe Local History, Wharncliffe True
Crime, Military Classics, Wharncliffe Transport,
Leo Cooper, The Praetorian Press, Remember When,
Seaforth Publishing and Frontline Publishing.

For a complete list of Pen & Sword titles
please contact
PEN & SWORD BOOKS LIMITED
47 Church Street, Barnsley, South Yorkshire,
S70 2AS, England
E-mail: enquiries@pen-and-sword.co.uk
Website: www.pen-and-sword.co.uk

ABBREVIATIONS

BA	Bundesarchiv
CNA	Canadian National Archives
IWM	Imperial War Museum
USMC	U.S. Marine Corps
USN	U.S. Navy
USNA	U.S. National Archives

AMERICA'S COMMANDOS
U.S. SPECIAL OPERATIONS FORCES OF WORLD WAR II AND KOREA

During World War II (1939-45) and the Korean War (1950-53), the U.S.A. deployed a diverse group of special operations forces (SOF) tasked with commando raids, supporting and initiating guerrilla raids, gathering intelligence, rescuing prisoners-of-war (POWs), and operating in environments normally hostile to military operations, such as under the sea or in the mountains. As is frequently the case with SOFs, opinions differed on the effectiveness of these units. Critics considered them a drain of highly motivated troops, who would have been more useful in conventional units, while supporters of SOFs lauded them as force-multipliers who tied down enemy troops and significantly eroded enemy morale.

In considering U.S. special operations during World War II, it is appropriate to look first at the U. S. Marines. Traditionally, the U.S.A.'s raiders and guerrilla fighters, the Marines during the 1930s had experimented with small raiding units deployed from rubber boats. British Commando operations in Europe during 1940 and 1941, many of which were typical 'Marine operations', had attracted substantial interest from the Marine Corps. In fact, United States Marine Corps (USMC) observers had made recommendations for similar units within the Corps.

These special Marine units were designated 'Raiders', the 1st Raider Battalion being formed in January, followed by the 2nd Raider Battalion in February 1942. Although most high-ranking Marines felt all Marines were capable of 'commando operations', the Raiders were given the mission of spearheading landings on 'inaccessible beaches', carrying out high-speed, hard-hitting raids, and organizing guerrilla operations.

The initial Raider operation took place in August 1942, when the 1st Raider Battalion landed on Tulagi as part of the Guadalcanal amphibious assault. A few days later, the 2nd Raider Battalion landed from submarines on Makin Atoll in a diversionary raid to pull Japanese reinforcements away from Guadalcanal.

Each Raider battalion was organized to allow flexibility, though the 2nd Battalion's organization proved more effective for small unit raids since it was based on three-man fire teams, three of which formed a squad. To grant devastating firepower, each Raider Battalion had about 200 Thompson sub-machine-guns in its inventory. On Guadalcanal, the 1st Raiders, reinforced by the Paramarines, helped drive Japanese defenders from around Henderson Field. They then broke repeated Japanese counterattacks on 'Bloody Ridge'. In November, the 2nd Raider Battalion also arrived on Guadalcanal.

In March 1943, the 1st and 2nd Raider Battalions, as well as the newly formed 3rd and 4th Raider Battalions, became part of the 1st Raider Regiment. In June 1943, some 150 Raiders landed on New Georgia to coordinate with coast watchers in preparation for Marine landings. Then, in September 1943, Raiders under a provisional 2nd Raider Regiment landed on Bougainville. By early 1944, the Marine Corps hierarchy had made its point that all Marines were elite raiding troops, making separate Raider units unnecessary. As a result, most Raiders were incorporated into the reconstituted 4th Marine Regiment.

Since they were drawn from already well-trained Marine Corps personnel, the Marine Parachute Units – the 'Paramarines' – also qualify as a special operations force. As early as May 1940, Major General Holcomb, the Commandant of the Marine Corps, had asked for plans to employ Marine parachute troops. Paramarines would be employed for reconnaissance and raiding, as spearheads to seize critical objectives, and as an independent guerrilla force behind enemy lines. Initially, each Marine regiment was to have an air-landing battalion, which incorporated a parachute company, thus requiring about 750 Paramarines for the entire Corps. In October 1940 the first 40 Marines began parachute training. By 1942, the Paramarine course included map reading, demolitions, scouting and patrolling, combat swimming, and weapons training, as well as parachuting.

The first combat for the Paramarines came on Guadalcanal alongside the 1st Raider Battalion. In September 1942, the 1st Parachute Battalion was withdrawn to New Caledonia for reindoctrination in jump techniques. They were joined by the 2nd Parachute Battalion early in 1943. When these units were later joined by the 3rd Parachute Battalion, the 1st Marine Parachute Regiment was formed. The 4th Parachute Battalion was also formed in the U.S.A. but was disbanded in January 1944.

During the Bougainville landings, the 2nd Parachute Battalion carried out a diversionary landing. Later, the 1st Parachute Battalion also landed on Bougainville. However, early in 1944, the Paramarines were disbanded and incorporated into other Marine units. Although two combat jumps reached the planning stage, none were actually made, at least partially due to lack of airlift capability in the Pacific.

The Marine Corps was not the only branch of the U.S. armed forces interested in the British Commandos. In 1942, U.S. Army Colonel Lucian Truscott had been sent to observe Commando training and arrange for some U.S. troops to receive the training. As a result of his observations, Truscott recommended that a U.S. commando unit be formed. Original plans called for personnel in this unit to serve for a while, then return to their regular units to share the expertise they had gained. U.S. Army raiding personnel were to be designated 'Rangers', based on the tradition of Rogers Rangers during the French and Indian Wars.

On 7 June 1942, the first Ranger unit was formed, mostly from U.S. troops training in Northern Ireland. From over 2000 initial volunteers, about 500 were selected. On 19 June this unit was officially designated 1st Ranger Battalion under Major William O. Darby. On 28 June, the new Rangers were sent to the Commando Depot at Achnacarry for training, after which they received amphibious training with the Royal Navy. In their first taste of combat, 50 Rangers accompanied Commandos on the Dieppe Raid. On 8 November 1942, the 1st Ranger Battalion landed in North Africa to seize artillery batteries defending a Tunisian harbor. For the next few months the 1st Rangers carried out raids to keep the Germans and Italians guessing where the major Allied thrust in Tunisia would strike. In April 1943, two more Ranger battalions were formed, with 1st Ranger Battalion veterans used as the core of the new units. To train the resulting 3rd and 4th Ranger Battalions, a training facility based on the Commando Training Center was built at Nemours.

Rangers next saw action on 10 July 1943 when the 1st and 4th Rangers under Darby spearheaded the Sicily landings. The 3rd Ranger Battalion also took part in the landings. Rangers were used again in the Salerno landings of 9 September 1943. During the Italian fighting, Rangers were often used for mountain operations; however, their amphibious skills were utilized when all three Ranger battalions landed at Anzio, where the 1st and 3rd Ranger Battalions were almost wiped out, with survivors assigned to the 1st Special Service Force. On 15 August 1944, the 1st and 3rd Ranger Battalions were inactivated, followed in October by the 4th Ranger Battalion.

After the Rangers had left Great Britain for North Africa and Italy, the U.S. wanted to retain a raiding capability. As a result, the 29th Provisional Ranger Battalion had been formed on 20 December 1942 with 1st Ranger Battalion veterans as a training cadre. Rangers were also sent through the Commando Training Depot and through amphibious training. They were then assigned to 4 Commando for combat experience in raids on Norway and France. The 29th Provisional Ranger Battalion was disbanded in October 1943, however, since additional Ranger units were due to arrive in Britain from the U.S.A.

The 2nd Ranger Battalion, activated in April 1943 under Major James Rudder, was put through training similar to the Commandos before deploying to England in November 1943, for training in cliff assaults in preparation for D-Day. The 5th Ranger Battalion, activated in September 1943, was deployed to England in January 1944. While awaiting D-Day, this battalion went through the Commando Training Depot.

On D-Day, the 2nd Ranger Battalion assaulted the Pointe du Hoc to silence German batteries interdicting both Omaha and Utah Beaches, while the 5th Ranger Battalion landed over the beachhead and drove to hook up with the 2nd Rangers. During the remainder of the war in Europe, Rangers were used in security operations and to assault strong points. The 5th Rangers did carry out one deep penetration infiltration mission to help expand the Saar bridgehead, but for the most part, Rangers were used as conventional infantry.

In the Pacific, Lieutenant General Walter Krueger wanted a Ranger unit for the assault on the Philippines, resulting in activation of the 6th Ranger Battalion in September 1944. After intensive training, the unit was deemed ready for Ranger missions, and in October, 1944, landed on islands guarding the entrance to Leyte Gulf. In January 1945, the 6th Rangers took part in the Luzon landings, but are probably best remembered for their part in the Cabanatuan POW Camp raid. Working with Philippine guerrillas and Alamo Scouts, the Rangers helped to free and evacuate Allied prisoners. The Alamo Scouts, which served directly under 6th Army G2, carried out what would later became another Ranger mission – long-range reconnaissance patrols. In scout teams of one officer and five or six enlisted men, the Alamo Scouts performed over 80 missions. The 6th Rangers were employed in clearing the mountainous areas of Luzon, and in May 1945 were used to capture Aparri Airfield on Luzon. In September 1945, the 6th Rangers left for occupation duty in Japan. Had the invasion of Japan been necessary, it is quite likely that the 6th Rangers, along with the 7th Rangers which were to have been formed from European Ranger vets and volunteers, would have spearheaded the landings.

Another American unit which operated behind enemy lines was the 5307th Composite Unit (Provisional), more commonly known as 'Merrill's Marauders'. After the success of the Chindits, the U.S.A. wanted a Long Range Penetration Unit of its own. Designated 'Galahad', this force drew volunteers from various U.S. commands. Upon arrival in India in October 1943, they trained under Orde Wingate and other Chindit veterans. In January 1944, the brigade-sized unit was designated the 5307th Composite Unit and prepared its 700 mules and horses for action, though aerial re-supply would have to provide anything the mules could not carry or the Marauders could not forage.

On 24 February 1944, the Marauders went into action carrying out an outflanking sweep to cut off retreating Japanese. Throughout March, the Marauders harassed retreating Japanese troops. Their final operation took place in May when they secured Myitkyina and its critical airfield near the Ledo Road. During their time in combat, Merrill's Marauders were in five major engagements and 30 minor ones. However, the Unit suffered such heavy casualties that it was inactivated on 10 August 1944. Many survivors were incorporated into the 475th Infantry Regiment (LRP, Special) in an attempt to retain the long-range penetration capability.

While Merrill's Marauders were trained to fight in the jungles of Burma, the U.S.A. also had two units trained to fight in the mountains and snow of Europe. One, the 1st Special Service Force, was originally formed to raid across frozen Northern Europe, using a tracked snow vehicle designated the T-24. In theory, this highly mobile brigade-sized force could tie down many times its numbers in German garrison troops to protect strategic targets.

Drawn from Canadian and American lumberjacks, trappers, guides, and other outdoorsmen; Force members were trained as commandos, mountain and ski troops, parachutists, and, eventually, amphibious raiders. Although it was decided the P-24 Weasel was impractical, the highly trained 1st Special Service Force did get a chance to put their special skills into practice in August 1943, the unit being sent to the Aleutians to help recapture Kiska. Then, during November 1943, the Force was sent to Italy where its training proved valuable in mountain fighting.

In February 1944, the Force was part of the landing force at Anzio with responsibilities for anchoring the Allied right flank. Force members carried out small unit night raids, which demoralized the German defenders. Later, the Force played a key role in the breakout from Anzio and drive towards Rome. After a period of rest, during the invasion of Southern France, the Force carried out amphibious landings on small islands containing German batteries. In December 1944 the unit was disbanded, but it had established a well-deserved reputation for toughness. Many observers, in fact, rated the 1st SSF the toughest U.S. unit of the war. Thus, when the U.S. Army Special Forces were formed, they paid homage to the Force by adopting its crossed arrowhead collar insignia and arrowhead-shaped shoulder insignia.

Even prior to the 1st SSF's formation for winter raiding, there had been interest in the War Department – at least partially generated by the success of Finnish ski troops in the Winter War – in creating a unit with mountain and ski skills. As a result, on 15 November 1941, the 1st Battalion (Reinforced), 87th Infantry Mountain Regiment was activated. Many early recruits were American skiers and mountaineers, including many from prominent families who had enjoyed sport skiing before the war. Eventually, a substantial number of European skiers and climbers who had emigrated to the U.S.A. would also serve with this unit.

As training progressed, ski and climbing equipment was developed as were military tactics on skis or when climbing. One early mission considered for the new unit was a raid on the Norwegian heavy water plant that was deemed critical to production of a Nazi atomic bomb. In fact, at one point Norwegian ski troops were incorporated into the 87th. In actuality, however, the unit's first action was the recapture of Kiska, though the Japanese had already evacuated.

In June 1943 the 10th Light Division (Alpine) was activated. Eventually, the division would include almost 5000 mules, about two-thirds of them assigned to four pack artillery battalions. On 7 November 1944 the official designation was changed to 10th Mountain Division, although the highly trained troops doubted they would ever see combat since the War Department had been holding the division in reserve, not sure where its skills could best be utilized. The slogging campaign in Italy, however, convinced General Mark Clark that he could use specially trained mountain troops.

The 10th Mountain Division arrived in Italy early in 1945 and was thrown into combat in the Apennines. One key mission was the seizure of RIva Ridge by the 86th Regiment from German Alpine troops after climbing a mountain face. Once the 86th had secured this objective, the 85th and 87th Regiments seized Mount Belvedere. The 10th also spearheaded the breakout into the Po Valley, seizing bridges across the Panaro River, then driving across the Po. When the war ended, 10th Mountain Division was in the foothills of the Alps. During its few months in combat, the 10th had suffered the heaviest casualties of any U.S. unit in the Italian campaign and had proven that the U.S.A. could field mountain troops every bit as good as the best European Alpine units.

Although many associate the Office of Strategic Services (OSS) with intelligence gathering, the OSS also had a special operations mission, primarily in raising and training guerrillas behind Axis lines. OSS personnel received training in such special ops skills as close combat, demolitions, and parachuting. As early as the invasion of North Africa, OSS agents were organizing local guerrilla and intelligence sources. In Sicily, OSS agents provided tactical intelligence and carried out raids against German communications and supply lines along the Italian coast. On Corsica, the OSS helped French guerrillas harass the Germans. By mid-1944 OSS operatives were working closely with partisan units throughout Italy, and by spring 1945 75 OSS teams had trained partisans supporting Allied advances.

Throughout 1944 and 1945, OSS agents operated in Greece and off the coast of Yugoslavia in support of local guerrillas. On D-Day and subsequently, other OSS teams known as Jedburghs parachuted in to work with the French Resistance in gathering intelligence and committing acts of sabotage to prevent German reinforcements and supplies from reaching defenders behind the beachhead. Between June and September 1944, a total of 276 Jedburghs jumped into occupied Europe. As the Allies advanced across Europe, Jedburgh-led partisans harassed retreating German forces. When larger teams were needed, the OSS committed its Operational Groups (OGs). Among the missions assigned to the OGs was preventing Germans from blowing critical bridges and destroying Norwegian hydroelectric plants.

While OSS teams were relatively successful in Europe, it was in Burma that OSS Detachment 101 established a legendary record in combat with the Kachin Rangers. Other OSS detachments operated in China, where they raised and trained Chinese 'Commandos', and in South-East Asia, where OSS agents were very impressed with Ho Chi Minh. Though the Central Intelligence Agency (CIA) is most widely accepted as having evolved from the OSS, the U.S. Special Forces with its guerrilla warfare mission also traces its origins to the OSS

American military personnel were also involved with the Philippine guerrilla movement but on a far more ad hoc basis than when the OSS was involved. Many of the Americans who served with the Philippine guerrillas had taken to the hills after the U.S. surrender. As the guerrilla movement grew, however, MacArthur's intelligence staff realized its value and arranged to send supplies and a few advisory personnel. Had MacArthur been more open to OSS operations in the Philippines it is quite likely this movement could have been even more effective in harassing the Japanese invaders and supporting U.S. landings.

U.S. Naval special operations forces evolved primarily in support of amphibious operations. Among these forces were the 'Beach Jumpers', which were used for deception during amphibious landings, and the Naval Combat Demolition Units, which were tasked with clearing obstructions in the way of landing craft. combat demolition units (CDUs) normally consisted of one officer and five enlisted personnel, a number determined by the capacity of the rubber boats used to approach the beach. The CDUs played an important part in landings in Europe and the Pacific, including on the Normandy beaches and in the Philippines. Later in the war, the CDUs evolved into the underwater demolition teams (UDTs) which saw action on Okinawa and elsewhere in the Pacific. The UDTs, who were the first U.S. combat swimmers to use fins, would have played a key role in the planned invasion of the Japanese home islands.

This vast array of U.S. SOFs which came into existence during World War II often carried out missions which contributed substantially to the war effort, especially in tying down Axis manpower through guerrilla activity or sabotage. Specialist units such as the 10th Mountain Division and UDTs also provided troops who could operate effectively in diverse environments. Some of these SOFs faded into legend at war's end, but others would evolve and see action during the Korean conflict.

The Rangers continued to serve in Korea but in Airborne Ranger Companies attached to each division to carry out raids and gather intelligence. These companies had a strength of five officers and 107 other ranks. Personnel were drawn from the ranks of airborne troops and given a six-week Ranger course. Some companies received an additional four weeks of mountain and winter warfare training at Fort Carson, Colorado. These Ranger companies were deactivated in 1951, but a Ranger Department was formed to train officers and NCOs in Ranger skills.

Within the army, the Special Forces were activated in June 1952 with the mission of carrying out unconventional warfare, particularly in Communist-dominated areas. In Korea, guerrilla units drawn from North Koreans were trained by the 8240th Army Unit to carry out raids and sabotage. After its formation, the 10th Special Forces

Group (SFG) sent personnel to the 8240th Army Unit. In 1953, the 77th SFG was activated, while the 10th SFG was rotated to Germany with the mission of raising guerrillas behind Soviet lines should the Cold War turn hot.

For sabotage raids along the North Korean coast, the Navy had a Special Operations Group comprised of a Marine Recon Company and UDT personnel. Though their strength had been cut back, the UDTs had been retained after World War II. Each unit consisted of about four officers and 50 other ranks. UDTs 1 and 3 were assigned to Coronado, California, and UDTs 2 and 4 were assigned to Little Creek, Virginia. These locations would remain the hubs of Navy special warfare for the next half-century. During the late 1940s, UDTs experimented with breathing apparatus, miniature submarines, and deployment from submerged submarines. In addition to the UDTs, the Navy also retained a small number of Beach Jumpers for deception operations during landings.

By the mid-1950s most of the units that would give the United States its formidable special warfare capability by the 1960s were in place. The UDTs were training for operations off the beach in preparation for their future role as Sea-Air-Land (SEAL) teams. The Army continued to train personnel in Ranger techniques, and Special Forces was already operating around the world. Marine Corps Recon troops were, as their title implies, trained for various reconnaissance missions as well as screening operations for larger Marine formations. As the second half of the 20th century brought increased guerrilla warfare and terrorism, U.S. special operations forces were poised to evolve to fit their new missions.

FOR FURTHER READING

Burhans, L. T. C. and Robert, D., *The First Special Service Force: A War History of the North Americans, 1942–1944*. Washington: Infantry Journal Press, 1947.

Burton, Hal, *The Ski Troops: A History of the 10th Mountain Division*. New York: Simon & Schuster, 1971.

Dunlap, Richard, *Behind Japanese Lines with the OSS in Burma*. New York: Rand McNally, 1979.

Dwyer, John, *Commandos from the Sea: The History of Amphibious Special Warfare in World War II and Korea*. Boulder, Colorado: Paladin Press, 1998.

Haas, Michael E., *In the Devil's Shadow: U. N. Special Operations During the Korean War*. Annapolis: Naval Institute Press, 2000.

Hogan, David W. Jr., *U.S. Army Special Operations in World War II*. Washington: Center of Military History, 1992.

Hopkins, James E.T., *Spearhead: A Complete History of Merrill's Marauder Rangers*. Baltimore: Galahad Press, 1999.

Ladd, James, *Commandos and Rangers of World War II*. London: Macdonald & Janes, 1978.

Updegraph, Charles L. Jr., *U.S. Marine Corps Special Units of World War II*. Washington: History and Museums Division, 1977.

Zedric, Lance Q., *Silent Warriors of World War II: The Alamo Scouts Behind Japanese Lines*. Ventura, California: Pathfinder Publishing, 1995.

The OSS Liberator pistol and an OSS arm dagger. (Author's Collection)

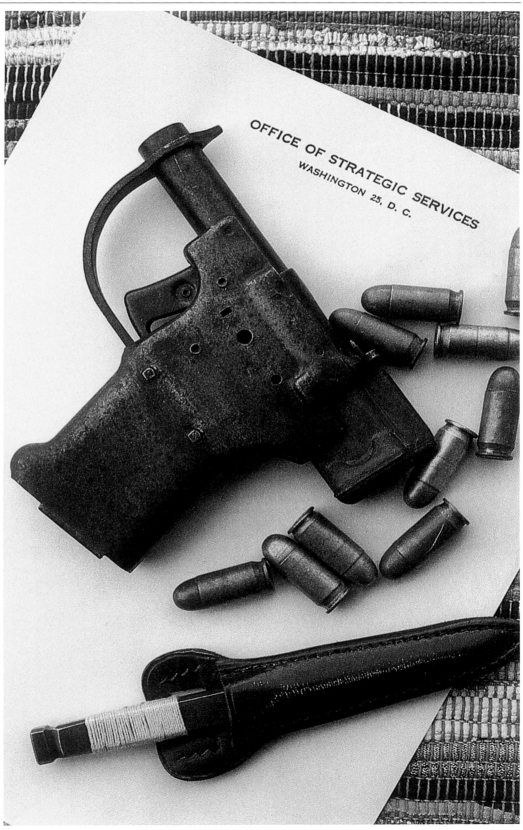

Opposite page: OSS dagger, OSS parachute wings, and OSS Colt automatic displayed on an OSS/SOE jump coverall. (Author's Collection)

Above: U.S. Navy Underwater Demolition Team members destroy North Korean fishnets during the Korean War to interdict the enemy's food supply. (USN)

Left: Danish Resistance Museum display of an underground workshop set up to build Sten guns. The OSS would have worked with resistance groups such as this. (Danish Resistance Museum)

Right: The First Special Service V-42 dagger and shoulder sleeve insignia. (Author's Collection)

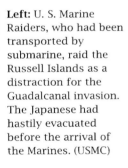

Left: U. S. Marine Raiders, who had been transported by submarine, raid the Russell Islands as a distraction for the Guadalcanal invasion. The Japanese had hastily evacuated before the arrival of the Marines. (USMC)

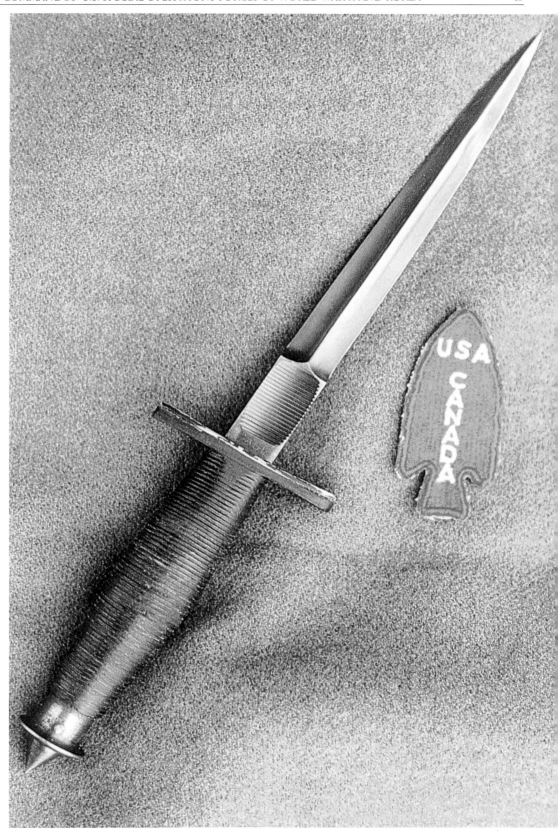

Left: A wounded 87th Mountain Infantry Division soldier and German soldier being treated at a 10th Mountain Division Battalion aid station. (USNA)

Above: A U.S. Navy Underwater Demolition Team frogman sharpens his knife prior to Operation Fishnet during the Korean War. (USN)

Above: A specially trained Raider Battalion hikes over rugged terrain on operations on Guadalcanal. The native guides were sympathetic to the Americans. (USMC)

Below: A group of Marine Raiders on Bougainville gather in front of a Japanese dugout on Camp Torokina in 1943. These tough jungle fighters have camouflage utilities and camouflage covers on their M1 helmets. They are armed with M-1903 Springfield and M1 Garand rifles. (USMC)

Above: U.S. Rangers undergoing realistic training in Britain with the Commandos. (USNA)

Below: U.S. Marine Raiders on Bougainville along with their 'Devil Dogs', which were usually Dobermans - although pictured here, in front, are two German shepherd dogs. (USMC)

Opposite page, top: Marines of the 2nd Raider Battalion slog through the mud in Torokina Area on Bougainville. (USMC)

Above: Marine Raiders fall back on the beach at Bougainville when boats appear offshore. They are equipped with an array of weapons: besides the M1 Garand, the two men in the left foreground have a Colt .45 automatics and what appears to be a Reising sub-machine-gun, while a soldier in the right background appears to be carrying a scoped sniping rifle. (USMC)

Left: Marine Raiders and Para Marines, who were operating together at this point, fire at Japanese snipers on Bougainville who are attempting to knock out the captured field gun (background, left) which has been turned against them. The Raiders and Marines have landed on a beach eight miles behind the Japanese lines to raid an enemy supply area. The boxes on the sand contain ammunition for the 37mm field piece. (USMC)

Opposite page, top: Rangers undergoing small-boat training in Britain illustrate the old-style M1917A1 U. S. Army helmet. The man in the right foreground carries a Browning automatic rifle. (IWM)

Opposite page, bottom: Rangers in training in Great Britain. The Browning automatic rifle was used by the Rangers much as the Commandos used the Bren Gun to give small units additional firepower. (IWM)

Above: A Ranger sergeant undergoing stalking training in Britain. His battalion identification has been obscured for security purposes. (IWM)

Opposite page: A U.S. Ranger sergeant sharpens his Fairbairn-Sykes Commando dagger. (IWM)

Above: Rangers undergoing realistic hand-to-hand combat training. The sheath is left on the combat knife to lower the chance of injury. (IWM)

Right: U.S. Rangers learn aggressive techniques of taking down an enemy sentry. (IWM)

Above: U.S. Rangers intermix with Commandos for the Dieppe Raid. They are equipped with a mixture of U.S. and British equipment. The Rangers wear the woolen cap comforter so popular with the Commandos. (IWM)

Left: U.S. Rangers with British Commandos on the Dieppe Raid still carry their Garand rifles since there was still a great shortage of weapons in the British Army at this time. (IWM)

Opposite page: The Fairbairn-Sykes dagger was popular with British, U.S., and Allied Special Operations forces during World War II. From left are illustrated the four basic World War II variations: the early 1st Pattern with S-guard, the Wilkinson marked 2nd Pattern, the unmarked and blackened 2nd pattern, and the ribbed hilt 3rd pattern. (Author's Collection)

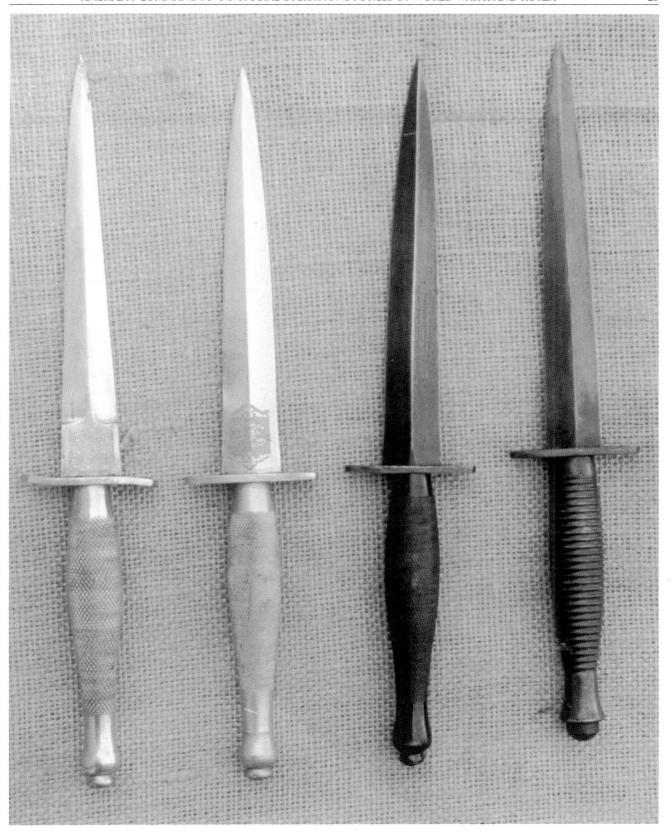

Opposite page: Major William O. Darby of the U.S. Rangers aboard the motorcycle he often rode. Darby chose to use the 1903 Springfield rifle rather than the later Garand. (USNA)

Above: U.S. Army Rangers boarding an assault craft for the D-Day landings in June 1944. (IWM)

Below: Rangers link up with Commandos on D-Day. The Ranger in the right foreground wears white reflective tape on his helmet so that the man behind him can keep position. Rangers still wear two reflective dots on their helmets known as 'Ranger eyes'. (IWM)

Above: Members of the 6th Ranger Battalion infiltrating toward the Cabanatuan Prison Camp to carry out a rescue. The short-billed HBT fatigue cap is worn by most of the men. Here, however, the Ranger in the left foreground wears the 'Daisy Mae' hat that was so popular in the Pacific Theater. (USNA)

Below: Members of the 6th Ranger Battalion on Luzon. (USNA)

Above: Members of Merrill's Marauders take a break along a trail in Burma. The mules were a key element of the 5307th Composite Groups supply system. (USNA)

Below: Members of Merrill's Marauders move along the Ledo Road. The point man is carrying a Gurkha Kukri as a combat and utility knife. (USNA)

Above: A member of Merrill's Marauders barters cigarettes for money with Chinese soldiers. (USNA)

Left: Brigadier General Merrill, commander of the 5307th Composite Group - a 'fighting general' armed with a rifle and carrying a full combat load. (USNA)

Opposite page, top: View of the mules and horses that became all too familiar to members of Merrill's Marauders. (USNA)

Opposite page, bottom: Field inspection for members of Merrill's Marauders in Burma. The Thompson SMG is laid out in the foreground and the M1 Carbine is carried by the soldier in the right foreground. Because it was light and allowed fast magazine changes, the M1 Carbine was very popular with the Marauders. (USNA)

Above: Members of Merrill's Marauders with their patrol dogs after the battle for Myitkying. (USNA)

Below: Members of Merrill's Marauders examine a captured Japanese Nambu light machine-gun. (USNA)

Opposite page: Members of Merrill's Marauders cross a bridge over the Chindwin in Burma while their mules swim across. (USNA)

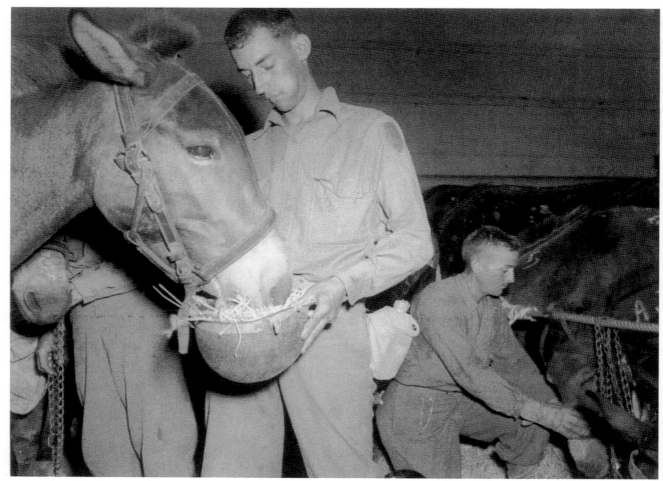

Opposite page, top: Members of Merrill's Marauders ford a river on operations in Burma. (USNA)

Opposite page, bottom: A mule handler finds his steel helmet very useful for feeding 5307th Composite Group mule and horses. (USNA)

Above: Air crew dropping supplies for Merrill's Marauders. (USNA)

Right: Members of the 5307th Composite Group on parade in January 1944. (USNA)

Above: Members of the 1st Special Service Force in jump helmets prepare to emplane for their first parachute jump. (USNA)

Left: A member of the 1st Special Service Force receives his parachute wings. The crossed arrow collar insignia was worn by the 1st SSF and later adopted by the U.S. Army Special Forces. (USNA)

Opposite page: Members of the 1st SSF undergoing mountain training. They are kitted out in reversible parkas. (USNA)

Opposite page, top: Members of the 1st SSF operating out of the Anzio Beachhead. (CNA)

Opposite page, bottom: A former hot-dog stand serves as the command post for the 1st Platoon of the 1st SSF at Anzio in April 1944. (CNA)

Above: At Anzio, members of the 1st SSF use a creek bed for cover as they man a Browning light machine-gun with improvised carrying handle. The helmets have field-expedient camouflage. (CNA)

Below: Members of the 1st SSF man a water-cooled Browning MG at the Anzio Beachhead. The soldier at right not only wears a double magazine pouch for his Colt automatic, but also carries additional spare rounds in cartridge loops. (CNA)

Opposite page, top: Members of the 1st SSF ready to set out on one of the night patrols that caused the Germans defending at Anzio to give them the name 'Black Devils'. The 1st SSF has a distinctive arrowhead shoulder patch with the legend 'U.S.A./CANADA'. (CNA)

Opposite page, bottom: Members of the 1st Special Service Force undergoing bayonet training at Fort Harrison,

Montana. Note the mountain/ski boots and that the Canadians have retained their 'Tams'. (CNA)

Above: Members of the 1st SSF who received Silver Stars and a DSC for operations at Anzio. (CNA)

Below: Members of the 1st SSF at the Anzio Beachhead. (CNA)

Above: Members of the 1st SSF man a mortar pit at the Anzio Beachhead. Leaning against the wall of the pit is a Johnson LMG. (CNA)

Left: Members of the 1st SSF with captured weapons at Anzio. (CNA)

Opposite page, top: Members of the 1st SSF infiltrate a minefield on a raid against the Germans out of the Anzio Beachhead. (USNA)

Opposite page, bottom: At left is Brigadier Robert Fredericks, commander of the 1st Special Service Force. The officer at right wears the 1st SSF arrowhead shoulder sleeve insignia. Both 'Force' men wear the M1943 field jacket. (USNA)

Opposite page, top: Brigadier General Fredericks of the 1st SSF (at right) meets with Lieutenant General Mark Clark, commander of the Fifth Army (second from right) and other generals as the Fifth Army prepares to move on Rome. Fredericks wears the distinctive 1st SSF V-42 stiletto in the sheath on his left hip and over the full-cut mountain trousers. (USNA)

Above: A 10th Mountain Division T-24 snow tractor pulling a cargo sled. (USNA)

Left: Members of the 10th Mountain Division with a 4.2 inch mortar in a mule pack. (USNA)

Opposite page, right: 10th Mountain Division ski troops ski cross-country towing cargo sleds. (USNA)

Opposite page, bottom: Members of the 10th Mountain Division transport a mortar and a pack howitzer up a mountain. (USNA)

Above: Members of the 3rd Battalion, 87th Mountain Infantry dig in during operations in the Abetia area of Italy in March 1945. (USNA)

Below: Members of the 10th Mountain Division fire a Browning light machine-gun at Germans along the Perretta-Moderna Highway in March 1945. (USNA)

Opposite page, top: A member of the 87th Mountain Infantry uses a Handy Talkie to report the position of a German mortar position. (USNA)

Opposite page, bottom: With their 75mm pack howitzers, members of the 616th Pack Artillery give fire support to

10th Mountain Division in February 1945. (USNA)

Above: A member of the 616th Pack Artillery loading a 75mm pack howitzer while in action in the Vincinetta area. (USNA)

Opposite page, top: 10th Mountain Division artillery observers descend Mount Serrasiccia via a tramway built by Company D, 126th Mountain Engineers. (USNA)

Opposite page, bottom: OSS training staff, including such well-known experts in close combat as W.E. Fairbairn (second from right, bottom row) and Rex Applegate (fourth from left, top row). (Rex Applegate)

Above: W. E. Fairbairn, who trained U.S. and British SOF during World War II, briefs an agent before he trains in the 'House of Horrors', a realistic live-fire shooting complex with pop-up targets and other training aids. (Dorothea Fairbairn)

Opposite page: An OSS Jedburgh equipped for a jump into occupied territory. A British-style paratroop helmet is worn along with what appears to be a Dennison smock. (USNA)

Above: OSS Jedburghs undergoing training in England. (USNA)

Below: OSS Jedburghs prior to em planing for a drop into Occupied Europe. The agents in the center and at right appear to be wearing the SOE jump coverall with pockets for pistol, gravity knife, and other equipment. (USNA)

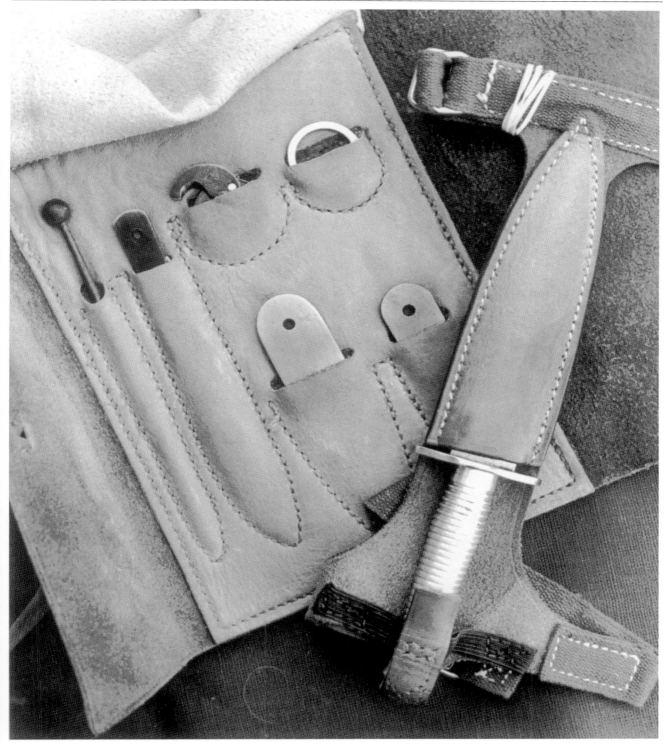

Opposite page, top: Jedburghs prepare to board a B-24 for a drop into Occupied Europe. (USNA)

Opposite page, bottom: Jedburgh teams were trained to work with local partisans, such as this one in Greece. (BA)

Above: OSS agents were trained to use a variety of edged weapons, including the miniature Fairbairn-Sykes knife shown here in an arm sheath, and the various thumb daggers, hat pins, and other clandestine blades. (Author's Collection)

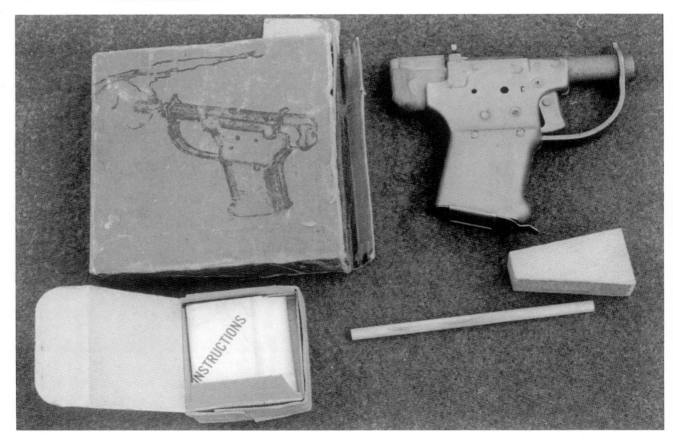

Opposite page, top: The Colt Pocket automatic was widely used by OSS personnel. Note the 'U.S. Property' marks. (Author's Collection)

Opposite page, bottom: The OSS Liberator pistol, which was designed to be dropped in occupied areas. The intent was that this simple weapon would be used to kill a German or Japanese soldier to obtain his more sophisticated weapon. Far more were dropped in Asia than in Europe, particularly in the Philippines. (Author's Collection)

Above: OSS-trained Kachin Rangers operating with Merrill's Marauders. (USNA)

Left: An OSS Jingpaw Ranger with family members. The shotgun was awarded to him for valor in combat. (USNA)

59

Left: Members of OSS Detachment 101 in Burma watch a Kachin ceremony given in honor of American personnel at Namtu in April 1945. The bush hat is worn by the OSS operative at right. (USNA)

Below: Head of the OSS 'Wild Bill' Donovan meets with other generals in the Mediterranean during 1943. In addition to Donovan, who is standing, other notables are Omar Bradley, seated second from right, and Theordore Roosevelt, Jr., second from left. Roosevelt would go on to win a Congressional Medal of Honor during the D-Day landings. (USNA)

Opposite page, top: An OSS radio operator receives a message from other OSS agents behind Japanese lines. He is pictured with three Kachin Rangers, one of whom is operating the hand crank power source. (USNA)

Opposite page, bottom: OSS Detachment 101 agents learn jungle skills in Burma. The diverse OSS armament includes a scoped M1903A4 Springfield, an M1 Carbine, and a Colt 45 automatic. (USNA)

Above: OSS personnel in Ceylon receive instruction in using the British 'Sleeping Beauty' breathing apparatus. (USNA)

Below: OSS personnel in Ceylon learn to use a one-man submarine. (USNA)

Left: OSS personnel in Ceylon. They are equipped with two types of breathing apparatus: at left, the Lambertsen unit; at right the 'Sleeping Beauty' unit intended for use in the one-man submarine. (USNA)

Opposite page, top: Members of the 1st Airborne Ranger Company chute up prior to a jump in Korea. (USNA)

Opposite page, bottom: Members of the 3rd Ranger Company check equipment for quietness prior to a patrol across the Imjin River in Korea. The Ranger third from right wears both Airborne and Ranger tabs over his 3rd Infantry Division insignia. The Ranger in left foreground is carrying a Browning automatic rifle. (USNA)

Left: Rangers of the 2nd Ranger Company bring their Browning light machine-gun into action in Korea. The U.S. Army became racially integrated after World War II and many of the black members of the Rangers in Korea were veterans of the World War II 555th Parachute Infantry. (USNA)

Above: Members of the 3rd Ranger Company gather intelligence about Chinese positions in the hills of Korea. The Ranger sniper is at left. (USNA)

Below: A member of the 3rd Ranger Company in Korea contacting support units on his AN/GRC-9 radio before pulling to higher ground. (USNA)

Above: Members of the 1st Airborne Ranger Company of the U.S. 8th Army carry out a practice jump in Korea during 1951. (USNA)

Below: LTC Edward Clayton, commanding officer of Underwater Demolition Team (UDT) 21, receives the first sword surrendered to Americans in Japanese home waters on 28 August 1945. (USN)

Opposite page, top: In October 1950, members of a UDT team paddle their rubber boats through Wonsan Harbor prior to exploding North Korean mines. (USN)

Opposite page, bottom: UDT team coming ashore from their rubber boat after traversing an enemy minefield in Korea in October 1950. (USN)

Opposite page, top: UDT members prior to exploding a North Korean minefield. Their equipment is very basic: mask, wet suit, fins, and Ka-Bar knife. (USN)

Opposite page, bottom: UDT members pull their 300lb rubber boat ashore at Wonsan, Korea, in October, 1950. (USN)

Left: UDT 'frogman' deploys from a speeding boat during Operation Fishnet in Korea during August 1952. (USN)

Below: Members of the 77th Special Forces Group undergo training in the mountains at Camp Hale and Fort Carson, Colorado, during 1955. (USNA)

Left: A member of the 77th SFG (ABN) demonstrates his equipment (1956). He wears a parachute helmet and the Special Forces shoulder sleeve insignia. (USNA)

Above: Members of the 77th Special Forces Group receive aerial re-supply while operating 'behind enemy lines' during an exercise in the Colorado Rockies during 1955. (USNA)

Below: A member of the 77th SFG (ABN) with a local 'guerrilla' during Operation Lodestar, an exercise carried out in the Colorado Rockies in October 1955. The green beret is worn here with parachute oval and flash. The patch is the World War II-era Airborne Command patch later used by the 77th SFG. (USNA)

Above: A member of the 77th SFG (ABN) positions his snow-camouflaged Browning machine-gun during mountain training at Camp Hale, Colorado, in 1956. (USNA)

Below: Members of the 77th SFG (ABN) parachute into Fort Hale, Colorado, during training exercises in 1955. (USNA)